DEC     2012

**Canada's Political Parties**

# THE BLOC QUÉBÉCOIS

## Douglas and Patricia Baldwin

**Weigl**

Published by Weigl Educational Publishers Limited
6325 10th Street SE
Calgary, Alberta
T2H 2Z9

Website: www.weigl.ca

Library and Archives Canada Cataloguing in Publication

Baldwin, Douglas, 1944-
        Bloc québécois / Douglas and Patricia Baldwin.

(Canada's political parties)
Includes index.
ISBN 978-1-77071- 694-0 (bound).--ISBN 978-1-77071-699-5 (pbk)

        1. Bloc québécois.  I. Baldwin, Patricia, 1946-  II. Title.
III. Series: Canada's political parties (Calgary, Alta.)

JL197.B56B35 2011     j324.271'0984     C2011-900814-9

Printed in the United States of America in North Mankato, Minnesota
1 2 3 4 5 6 7 8 9 0  15 14 13 12 11

072011
WEP040711

Project Coordinator: Heather Kissock
Design: Terry Paulhus

Photograph Credits
CP Images: pages 6, 7T, 12, 13TL, 14, 15BL, 15BR, 16, 17TR, 17BR, 19BR, 21BL, 21BR, 24TM, 24TR, 25T, 25BR, 27; Dreamstime: page 4; Getty Images: pages 7B, 9L, 10, 11, 13TR, 13BL, 13BR, 15TL, 15TR, 17TL, 17BL, 18, 19TL, 19TR, 19BL, 20, 21TL, 21TR, 24TL, 24M, 24B, 25ML, 25BL, 26; Library and Archives Canada: pages 8, 9R, 9B.

Every reasonable effort has been made to trace ownership and to obtain permission to reprint copyright material. The publishers would be pleased to have any errors or omissions brought to their attention so that they may be corrected in subsequent printings.

We acknowledge the financial support of the Government of Canada through the Canada Book Fund for our publishing activities.

# CONTENTS

# Overview of Canada's Political Parties

Political parties in Canada are made up of people with similar beliefs who have joined together to accomplish specific goals. To achieve these goals, the party attempts to elect enough members to gain control of the government.

Political parties are central to our political system. In their attempts to win elections, parties propose a series of social, economic, and political policies called the party platform. The election campaign then attempts to convince the people to vote for candidates who support these beliefs. This process provides the people with a way of expressing their opinions and of holding the winning party accountable for its actions.

## Beginnings

The first Canadian political parties started in central Canada in the 1820s and 1830s. They were created to ensure that the people's wishes were presented to the British governor who ruled the **colonies**. The achievement of **responsible government** in the late 1840s paved the way for the emergence of party politics as we know it today. When Canada became a nation in 1867, there was only the Liberal Party and the Conservative Party. These two parties dominated politics until the 1920s. The rise of the Progressive Party in the 1920s, and the emergence of the Co-operative Commonwealth Federation (CCF) and the Social Credit parties in the 1930s gave voters more choices through which to express their concerns. However, these "third" parties never seriously challenged the power of the two major parties.

This situation changed, however, in the 1980s. The Reform Party began in 1987 as an alternative to the Progressive Conservative Party. In 2000, it transformed into the Canadian Alliance, which then merged with the Progressive Conservative Party in 2003 to form the Conservative Party of Canada. Today, the Conservative Party, Liberal Party, New Democratic Party (NDP), Green Party, and Bloc Québécois compete to dominate Canadian politics.

🍁 The Parliament Buildings in Ottawa have been the centre of Canadian politics since 1867.

# The Bloc Québécois—
# Its Beliefs and Philosophy

The Bloc Québécois' main goal is to create the **sovereign nation** of Québec, independent from Canada. In other words, it campaigns to have Québec leave the country.

The Bloc Québécois has one over-riding philosophy—Québec can only achieve true greatness if it is an independent nation. It thus seeks to create the conditions necessary for the **secession** of Québec from Canada. In the House of Commons, the Bloc seeks to protect Québec's interests on a federal level.

**Policy Statement**

In 2008, the Bloc presented its policy statement. The following passages indicate some of the party's core philosophies:

"In Québec, we share values that unite and define us, including the primacy of French as the common public language, the crucial role that culture plays in our national life …."

"Québec culture is vitally important for our people who represent only 2 percent of North America's population. Other parties consider Québec culture a regional component of Canadian culture; consequently, the Bloc Québécois is the only true ally of Québec culture."

"In recent decades, Québec has developed an approach to integrate immigrants into the Québec nation. This open approach goes against Canada's multiculturalism ideology, which encourages various communities to live in isolation. The Bloc Québécois is the only party that defends Québec's approach, while the other Canadian parties defend Canadian multiculturalism."

## Registering a Political Party

**1.** Political parties do not have to be registered with the government. However, registered parties can provide tax receipts for donations, thus saving the donors money. An official party can place its name beneath its candidates' names on the ballot.

**2.** To be registered, a party must:
- Have statements from at least 250 individuals who are qualified to vote (i.e. 18 years old and a Canadian citizen) indicating that they are party members
- Endorse (sponsor) at least one candidate in a general election or a by-election
- Have at least three officers, in addition to the party leader, who live in Canada and are eligible to vote
- Have an auditor
- Submit a copy of the party's resolution appointing its leader
- Have an agent who is qualified to sign contracts
- Submit a letter stating that the party will support one or more of its members as candidates for election

**3.** The party's name, abbreviation, or logo (if any) must not resemble those of any other party and must not include the word "independent." Once the Chief Electoral Officer has verified the party's application (confirming that 250 electors are members of the party and that the party has met all the other requirements), and is satisfied that the party's name and logo will not be confused with those of another registered or eligible party, he or she will inform the party leader that the party is eligible for registration.

Source: Elections Canada

# Bloc Québécois Leaders

The Bloc Québécois has only been in existence for about 20 years. As a result, it has had few leaders in its short history. Still, these people have made an impact on the political landscape not only in Québec, but throughout the country.

| Bloc Québécois Leaders | |
|---|---|
| NAME | TERM |
| Lucien Bouchard | 1990–1996 |
| Gilles Duceppe | 1996 |
| Michel Gauthier | 1996–1997 |
| Gilles Duceppe | 1997–2011 |
| Vivian Barbot | 2011–present |

**FIRST PARTY LEADER**

## LUCIEN BOUCHARD (1938-)

Bouchard was born in Saint-Cœur-de-Marie, Québec, in 1938. He obtained a BA and a law degree at Laval University and practiced law until 1985. In 1998, Prime Minister Brian Mulroney assigned Bouchard to the Conservative Cabinet as Minister of the Environment. Bouchard resigned from the party in 1990 and formed the Bloc Québécois. He became premier of Québec six years later and resigned from the position in 2001. He now works as a lawyer in Montreal.

In 1994, Bouchard had to have a leg amputated when he contracted a disease called necrotizing fasciitis.

## MICHEL GAUTHIER
### 1950-

Gauthier was born in Québec City in 1950. In 1981, he was elected to the provincial government as a member of the **Parti Québécois**. In 1993, he joined the Bloc Québécois in the House of Commons. When Bouchard left the Bloc to become premier of Québec, Gauthier was appointed party leader. Gauthier was unpopular with many party members for his apparent conservative views. When several members of the party threatened to revolt, Gauthier resigned in March 1997. He remained as the Bloc house leader in the House of Commons until he retired from politics in 2007.

Following his political career, Gauthier became the host of a television news show in Québec.

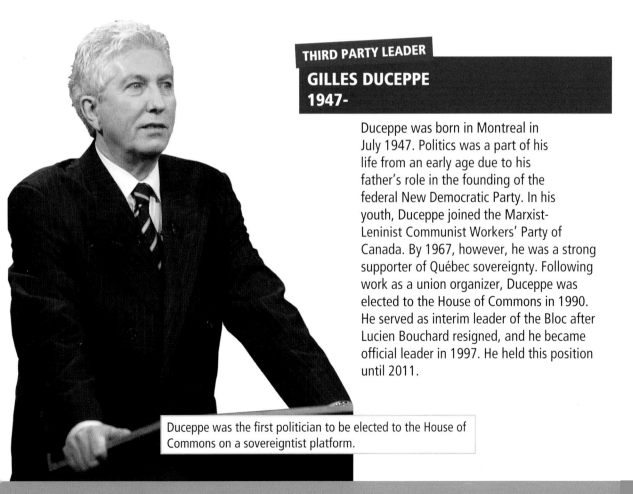

## GILLES DUCEPPE
### 1947-

Duceppe was born in Montreal in July 1947. Politics was a part of his life from an early age due to his father's role in the founding of the federal New Democratic Party. In his youth, Duceppe joined the Marxist-Leninist Communist Workers' Party of Canada. By 1967, however, he was a strong supporter of Québec sovereignty. Following work as a union organizer, Duceppe was elected to the House of Commons in 1990. He served as interim leader of the Bloc after Lucien Bouchard resigned, and he became official leader in 1997. He held this position until 2011.

Duceppe was the first politician to be elected to the House of Commons on a sovereigntist platform.

Louis-Joseph Papineau was the leader of the Parti Patriote and played a key role in the rebellions of 1837.

# Separatist Beginnings, 1763–1837

**The roots of Québec's separatist movement are older than Canada itself.**

The roots of Québec's separatist movement are older than Canada itself. They have been brewing since Great Britain defeated France in the Seven Years' War and assumed control of **New France** in 1763. The British issued the 1763 Royal Proclamation, which was an effort to **assimilate** the French into British culture. The proclamation allowed French Canadians to remain Roman Catholics and to speak French. However, the British encouraged British settlers to come to Québec and began building Protestant schools. Their expectation was that the French would get accustomed to British Protestant customs and principles and eventually assume these principles themselves.

The plan to assimilate the French met with little success. In 1791, as part of the **Constitution** Act, the French were given their own colony, known as Lower Canada. At first, this appeared to give the French the freedom to maintain their culture. However, over time, British merchants and settlers began to gain influence in Lower Canada. Tensions rose between British and French again. The French Canadians created their own political party, the Parti Patriote, to help protect French-Canadian culture, which they believed was endangered by the British elite who lived in Québec and now controlled the government. Their attempt to achieve a more **democratic** government ended in armed rebellion and defeat.

Following the rebellions of 1837, Britain sent Lord Durham to Canada to assess the situation in Lower Canada and make recommendations to resolve it. Durham blamed the French Canadians for the rebellions. He did not understand how deeply French Canadians treasured their language and traditions and thought that they were too uneducated to govern themselves. Since he believed that British ways were superior to French ways, Durham recommended that French Canadians be assimilated.

# WAS DURHAM CORRECT IN HIS ANALYSIS?

The British government asked Lord Durham to find the reasons for the 1837 rebellions and make recommendations. Durham blamed the French Canadians. He wrote, "I found two nations warring in the bosom of a single state." He thus recommended that French Canadians be assimilated by uniting the two colonies.

## DURHAM

Durham thought that the French Canadians were too uneducated to govern themselves and were easily misled by troublemakers. Assimilation to British ways, he argued, would benefit the French Canadians. Living side-by-side with the English, the French would learn British ways of living and lose their sense of identity as a separate people.

## FRENCH CANADIANS

The real cause of the rebellion was that a minority, the British, controlled the majority for its own gain. French Canadians wanted to preserve their way of life, and they wanted the British to respect their rights. The rebellions were staged to assert the rights of the French Canadians and retain their culture.

## THE RESULT

Great Britain united Upper and Lower Canada in 1841. English was made the only official language, although French was permitted in certain situations. French Canadians focussed on developing their culture and prospered.

### Lord Durham's Report contained two major recommendations.

1. Unite Upper and Lower Canada into one province so that English-speaking people would make up the majority.
2. Separate British affairs from local Canadian affairs by granting responsible government. After reviewing the report, the British government agreed only to the creation of a single province. Lower and Upper Canada became the United Province of Canada.

As a result of his recommendations, Lord Durham is sometimes called the father of responsible government in Canada.

# Growing Tensions, 1841–1917

Confederation was supposed to give French Canadians more control over their rights.

The Durham Report led to the Act of Union in 1841, which united Upper and Lower Canada under one government. By the 1860s, however, it was almost impossible to govern the combined colony. Petty jealousies, personality conflicts, and religious and ethnic differences resulted in a political deadlock. Between 1857 and 1864, there were three elections and five different governments. Since no party could hold power for long, the government passed few important laws. Tensions rose between French and English as each cancelled the other out in government decisions.

Separating the colony became a point of discussion once again. This time, however, the separation was actually part of a plan to unite all of Great Britain's North American colonies. Confederation separated the United Province of Canada into Ontario and Québec but made them part of a larger whole that included Nova Scotia and New Brunswick.

Confederation was supposed to give French Canadians more control over their rights. However, in the next four decades or so, several French-English disputes arose that appeared to result in the majority of English Canadians getting their way. The North-West Resistance, for example, led to the hanging of Louis Riel, a French-Catholic Métis. The Manitoba Schools Act in 1890 removed public funding for a Roman Catholic, and mostly French-attended, school system. Canada's participation in the Boer War also led to tension.

The tensions continued into the 20th century. During World War I, the issue of **conscription** divided Canada. Unlike English Canadians, French Canadians had no ties with Great Britain. They did not want to fight in a war they felt was about British supremacy. When conscription was passed in 1917, there were riots in Montreal. One demonstrator was killed. More rioting also took place in Québec City. Once again, French Canadians felt that the majority had over-ridden the desires of the minority.

Issues such as these strengthened the resolve of those individuals who wanted Québec to have as much control over its own affairs as possible.

🍁 Canadian casualties in World War I totaled more than 200,000. Approximately 56,500 of these casualties were fatal.

# CANADA IN THE BOER WAR

With the discovery of diamonds and gold in South Africa, tensions grew between the original Dutch settlers, or Boers, and the English until the Boer War began in 1899. The British government asked each of its colonies to send troops. This request divided French and English Canadians and threatened to split Canada apart.

## YES, SEND TROOPS

English-Canadians demanded that the Canadian government send troops to South Africa to help Great Britain defeat the Boers. Many English Canadians believed that closer Empire ties would make Canada a more important country and speed its evolution to independence. The war, they claimed, pitted British freedom, justice, and civilization against Boer "backwardness."

## NO, DO NOT SEND TROOPS

Why did the world's most powerful country need Canada's help to defeat a few Boers? Many French Canadians identified with the Boers. Like them, the Boers were surrounded by their conquerors, a people with a different language, culture, and religion. Becoming part of a larger British empire would make French Canadians an even smaller minority.

## THE RESULT

The government compromised. It agreed to equip and send Canadian volunteers to South Africa. However, once in South Africa, the Canadian troops would become Great Britain's responsibility. In the next three years, 7,368 Canadians served overseas. When the war ended in 1902, about 250 Canadians had died of disease or in battle.

**The turn of the 20th century was a time of international tension. French Canadians often felt the weight of British influence when conflicts broke out.**

1. Prior to World War I, the British fought the Boer War in South Africa. Against the wishes of French Canadians, Canada sent volunteer forces to fight alongside the British.
2. Great Britain and Germany embarked on an **arms race**. Germany took the lead with the restructuring of its navy. Great Britain asked Canada to provide money to help it build its naval forces. French Canadians protested, but the Canadian government created its own navy and agreed to loan it to Great Britain if needed.

More than 7,000 Canadians served in the Boer War. It was the first time that Canadian troops were sent overseas to fight.

🍁 The War Measures Act could be invoked whenever the Canadian government felt that Canada was under threat of war or invasion. The act was used during both world wars, but the FLQ crisis was the only time it was used to control a domestic crisis.

# The Quiet Revolution, 1960–1970

By 1960, a new generation of Québecers was expressing frustration with its position within Canada. Francophones felt like second-class citizens in their own province. Most of the higher paying jobs in the province went to Anglophones, and the language of business was English. The vast majority of immigrants to Québec learned English, not French. Most of the largest companies were owned by English Canadians or Americans. The Francophones demanded equality with English Canadians. "It's time for a change" was the Liberal Party's slogan in the 1960 provincial election.

With the Liberal victory, la Révolution Tranquille, or the Quiet Revolution, began. It was a period of modernization. Under the slogan "*maître chez nous*," or "masters in our own house," the provincial government began to plan programs that encouraged the growth of the province and its people. It was during this period that Québec also stated its desire for "special status" within Canada so that Québecers could become "masters in their own house."

> **Francophones felt like second-class citizens in their own province.**

The Quiet Revolution turned bloody in 1963. **The Front de Libération du Québec (FLQ)** believed that it could "free" Québec through violent revolution. Between 1963 and 1970, the FLQ was responsible for more than 200 bombings. In October 1970, FLQ members kidnapped British diplomat James Cross from his Montreal home and stated that he would be executed if their demands were not met. Five days later, the terrorists kidnapped Pierre Laporte, the Québec minister of labour and immigration.

Prime Minister Pierre Trudeau invoked the **War Measures Act** and put the nation under temporary **martial law**. On October 17, police found the body of Pierre Laporte in the trunk of an abandoned car. Laporte's kidnappers were later arrested and James Cross was found and released. Five FLQ terrorists were flown to Cuba in 1970 as part of a deal in exchange for James Cross' life.

# USING THE WAR MEASURES ACT

When the FLQ kidnapped James Cross and Pierre Laporte, Québec was in crisis mode. The incident had international impact and threatened to create tensions in foreign relations. The provincial government asked the federal government to help gain control of the situation. Invoking the War Measures Act was one way to do this, but it could be perceived by some to be extreme. Prime Minister Pierre Trudeau had to decide if invoking the War Measures Act would be the most effective way to end the terrorism.

## YES

Québecers feared that the FLQ would strike again. The quickest way to get the problem under control was to fight force with force. Having a strong military presence in Québec would also reassure Québecers that the federal government was making a concerted effort to protect them and fight the terrorism.

## NO

The Act gave the police power to search, question, and arrest suspects without cause. Some Canadians opposed it as a threat to civil liberties. Tommy Douglas, the leader of the NDP, declared, "I say to the government that we cannot protect democratic freedom by restricting, limiting and destroying democratic freedom."

## THE RESULT

When Trudeau invoked the War Measures Act to bring the situation under control, 92 percent of the Canadian population supported his decision. Almost 500 people were arrested and held in custody for up to three weeks without being charged. Many were imprisoned merely on suspicion. Most were later released.

**Maître chez nous**

**During the Quiet Revolution, the Québec government took several steps to make the province more autonomous.**

1. It modernized the education system, with an emphasis on making education more available and affordable.
2. It **nationalized** hydroelectric power.
3. It assumed control of hospitals and health care from the Catholic Church.
4. It unionized the civil service.

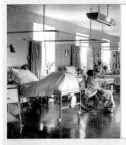

After taking over the health care system in Québec, the provincial government worked with the federal government to introduce a universal health care program for Québecers.

Prior to the Quiet Revolution, very few students were graduating from high school. Most quit while in junior high. When the Québec government took control of the province's education system, it made school attendance compulsory until students were 16 years of age.

# A Distinct Society, 1968–1987

The end of the FLQ crisis did not mean the end of separatism. Many Québécois still believed in achieving independence, but by lawful means. René Lévesque was one such person. Lévesque became frustrated with the non-separatist attitude of the Liberal Party and formed the Parti Québécois in 1968. Eight years later, Lévesque became premier of Québec and announced that he would hold a **referendum** in 1980 on Québec's future. Québecers were asked to vote "oui" or "non" on whether they wished to give the Québec government the "mandate to negotiate **sovereignty-association** with Canada."

Nearly 60 percent of Québecers voted against the plan. The defeat of the referendum led to a temporary decline in separatist support. The pendulum now swung to federalists like Pierre Trudeau who wanted Québec to have more influence in the federal government.

In 1982, Prime Minister Trudeau and the provincial premiers agreed to **patriate** Canada's Constitution from Great Britain. Canada, not Great Britain, would control the Constitution. Québec was the only Canadian province not to approve of the Constitution Act. Premier Lévesque claimed that the new Constitution had been imposed on Québec against its will and did not reflect its needs. Although Québec was bound by the new Constitution, French Canadians remained unhappy.

When Brian Mulroney became prime minister in 1984, he was determined to make changes in the Constitution that would satisfy Québec. Three years later, Mulroney and the 10 provincial leaders met at Meech Lake, Québec, to discuss constitutional changes. Their agreement was called the Meech Lake Accord. Among its provisions, the Accord recognized the province of Québec as a distinct society within Canada and awarded the provinces more power from the federal government. To become law, the Accord had to be **ratified** by Parliament and the legislatures of each province. Although the Parti Québécois opposed the Meech Lake agreement because it did not grant Québec enough autonomy, Québec agreed to the Accord in June 1987. That left three years for the other provinces to ratify the Accord. When Manitoba and Newfoundland and Labrador failed to approve the agreement within the required time, the Meech Lake Accord failed.

**The Meech Lake Accord recognized Québec as a distinct society within Canada.**

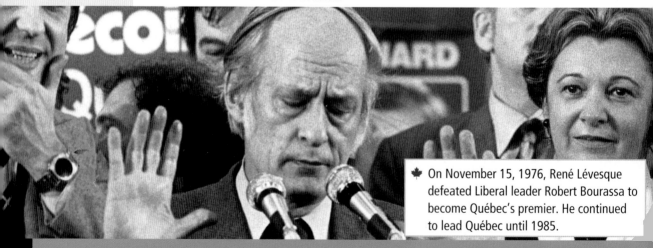

❦ On November 15, 1976, René Lévesque defeated Liberal leader Robert Bourassa to become Québec's premier. He continued to lead Québec until 1985.

# APPROVING MEECH LAKE

When Prime Minister Mulroney organized the meeting at Meech Lake, his main goal was to resolve the issues Québec had with the Canadian Constitution. Québec felt undervalued and wanted its cultural identity formally acknowledged. The Meech Lake Accord was to do this by stating that Québec was a distinct society within Canada. The "distinct society" clause caused an uproar throughout the country. Lawyers, politicians, and the Canadian public struggled to understand what the implications of this clause were and if it was giving Québec unspoken powers that no other province had.

## YES TO THE ACCORD

Québec's refusal to accept Canada's new constitution in 1981 made it feel separated from the rest of Canada. The Meech Lake Accord, said Mulroney, would build "a stronger Canada for all Canadians." The Accord, which represented Québec's minimum demands, would bring it back into the "constitutional family."

## NO TO THE ACCORD

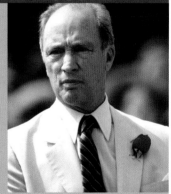

Former Prime Minister Pierre Trudeau claimed that Québec was no more distinct than many other places in the nation. The Accord, others said, weakened federal government powers while giving too much power to the provincial governments. Aboriginal Canadians argued that they should also be recognized as distinct.

## THE RESULT

When the Meech Lake Accord failed, Québec viewed the failure as a refusal by the rest of Canada to recognize its uniqueness. The Accord's failure led to the creation of the Bloc Québécois.

**The Meech Lake Accord included the following concessions to Québec.**

1. The Accord confirmed constitutional recognition of Québec as a "distinct society."
2. It required all provinces to consent to constitutional amendments.
3. It provided a formula to amend the Constitution.
4. It gave the provinces participation in making appointments to the Supreme Court of Canada and required that the court contain at least three judges from Québec.
5. It gave the provinces more control over immigration.

Québec Premier Robert Bourassa took part in the parliamentary commission on the Meech Lake Accord in May 1987.

Demonstrators showed their support for the Accord during the constitutional talks that took place in Ottawa in 1990.

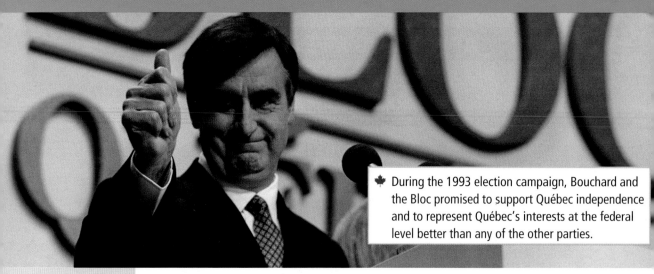

During the 1993 election campaign, Bouchard and the Bloc promised to support Québec independence and to represent Québec's interests at the federal level better than any of the other parties.

# The Founding Years, 1990–1992

Québec viewed the failure of the Meech Lake Accord as a refusal by the rest of Canada to recognize its uniqueness. Lucien Bouchard, who had resigned from the Progressive Conservative Party to protest a change to the accord's distinct society clause, started recruiting other unhappy Québec members of Parliament (MPs) when the Meech Lake Accord failed. In a few weeks, he formed an informal coalition of Conservative and Liberal MPs from Québec. The coalition became known as the Bloc Québécois.

In August 1990, Bloc candidate Gilles Duceppe was elected in a Montreal riding by-election and became the first Bloc Québécois MP to be elected to the House of Commons. Since the Bloc was not registered as a federal political party, Duceppe ran as an independent. The Bloc Québécois became an official party the next year. The founding convention attracted 600 supporters and elected Lucien Bouchard as its first leader.

The first test for the Bloc Québécois was the 1992 referendum on the Charlottetown Accord. This was Mulroney's second attempt to get Québec to accept Canada's Constitution.

**The Bloc Québécois became an official party on June 15, 1991.**

After months of discussion, Mulroney and the provincial premiers reached an agreement while they were in Charlottetown, PEI. Unlike the Meech Lake Accord, the Charlottetown Accord was to be ratified by a national referendum. Québec premier Robert Bourassa threatened to hold a vote on separatism if the country did not meet Québec's demands by accepting the Accord.

The referendum question was: "Do you agree that the Constitution of Canada should be renewed on the basis of the agreement reached on August 28, 1992?" To be approved, a majority of voters had to answer "Yes," and a majority of voters in each province had to agree.

The Conservative, Liberal, and NDP parties supported the Accord. It was opposed by the Bloc Québécois, Jacques Parizeau's Parti Québécois, and the western Reform Party. The Bloc argued that the Accord did not give Québec enough powers.

On October 26, 1992, Canadians rejected the Accord by 55 to 45 per cent. In Québec, 55 per cent voted no.

# THE CHARLOTTETOWN ACCORD

One of the main concerns that came out of the Meech Lake Accord negotiations was that the Canadian public was not asked for its input on the issue. When Prime Minister Mulroney decided to try again with the Charlottetown Accord, it was decided that the agreement be put to the people in a national referendum. It was up to Canadians to decide whether the Accord would be good for Canada.

## YES TO THE ACCORD

Since the failure of the Meech Lake Accord, tensions in the country had risen to an all-time high. Québec separatism was becoming a firm reality. The Accord had several flaws, but it would acknowledge Québec as a distinct society and calm the situation. Canada would remain in one piece.

## NO TO THE ACCORD

There was still no firm definition for "distinct society." While some people felt the term gave Québec special powers, Québec argued that the accord did not give the province enough powers. The accord had the potential to radically change the way in which the federal government operated by giving most of the power to the provinces.

## THE RESULT

On October 26, 1992, Canadians rejected the Accord. Early the next year, Mulroney announced his retirement. In the subsequent 1993 election, the Bloc Québécois won 54 seats, and Lucien Bouchard became the leader of the Official Opposition.

Charlottetown Accord

**The Charlottetown Accord was a wide-ranging agreement that outlined which powers the federal and provincial governments would have.**

1. It recognized Québec as a distinct society.
2. It stated that Québec would never have fewer than one-quarter of all the seats in the House of Commons.
3. It agreed that the federal power to veto provincial laws would be limited.
4. Matters relating to French language culture would require approval by a majority in the Senate as well as a majority of francophone senators.

Demonstrations were held across Québec in support of the provincial stance on the distinct society clause.

Québec currently has 75 of the 301 seats in the House of Commons. This is 25 percent of the seats.

# Gaining Ground, 1993–1997

In February 1993, with his popularity at its lowest, Mulroney retired from politics and was replaced by Kim Campbell. In the election that year, the Conservative Party suffered the worst defeat in Canadian history. When Canadians woke up the morning after the election, many were stunned to learn that the Bloc Québécois had captured the second most seats and was now the Official Opposition.

As the Official Opposition, the Bloc enjoyed considerable privileges, including more funding than other opposition parties and the right to speak first after all government announcements. As a result, the Bloc ensured that issues that concerned Québec dominated Question Period—often to the irritation of the other parties.

Partly because of the failure of the Charlottetown Accord, Jacques Parizeau's separatist Parti Québécois won the 1994 Québec provincial election. On October 30, 1995, Québec voters were asked to give the Québec government permission to negotiate a new agreement with the rest of Canada. Although the agreement would involve political independence, Québec would maintain economic ties with Canada.

Initially, the "yes" side did poorly. However, when Bouchard and the Bloc assumed control of the campaign in the last three weeks, the success of the referendum began to seem like a real possibility. Ultimately, the "no" side squeaked out a narrow 50.6 to 49.4 percent victory. A record 92 percent of the electorate voted.

In January 1996, Parizeau resigned from the Parti Québécois. He was replaced by Lucien Bouchard. Michel Gauthier was appointed leader of the Bloc by the party's leaders rather than by a vote of all the party's members, which weakened his control of the party. When party members threatened to revolt, Gauthier resigned in March 1997. He was succeeded by Gilles Duceppe.

> **When Canadians woke up the morning after the election, many were stunned to learn that the Bloc Québécois was now the official opposition.**

🍁 In the days leading up to the 1995 referendum, demonstrations were held in Québec and across the country to persuade Québec to remain part of Canada.

# SHOULD Québec SEPARATE?

The failure of the Meech Lake and Charlottetown Accords combined with the rise of the Bloc Québécois helped to create a strong separatist movement in Québec. While there were benefits to being part of a larger political entity, many Québecers felt that they did not receive enough support federally to make being Canadian worthwhile.

## YES, SEPARATE

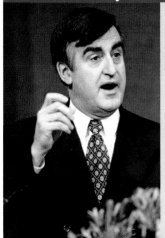

The Yes side stated that the existing situation did not allow Québec to attain its own goals. Bouchard declared, "We have… all the ingredients of a people, of a nation and … a distinct collectivity with the flavour and the nature and the aspirations of a people, of a nation."

## NO, STAY IN CANADA

The No side focused on how a separate Québec would not bring prosperity. Jean Chrétien stated, "The end of Canada would be … the end of a country that has made us the envy of the world. Canada is not just any country. It is unique. It is the best country in the world."

## THE RESULT

It was a very close vote, but Québecers voted "no" to separation. However, it was important to note that approximately 60 percent of Francophones voted for separation. There was still work to be done in Québec to gain their support for a united Canada.

Terms of Separation

**The Québec government recommended the following terms if it became separate and formed a partnership with Canada.**

1.  It would continue to use the Canadian dollar as its currency.
2.  Québec citizens be given **dual citizenship**.
3.  It would maintain its economic ties to Canada.

The promise to continue using the Canadian currency was meant to assure Québecers that, in the event of separation, Québec would maintain an economic relationship with Canada.

While the Parti Québécois worked to assure Québecers that secession would not completely sever the province's ties with Canada, Jacques Parizeau made several comments during the campaign that implied otherwise. Ultimately, it is believed that these comments hurt the campaign.

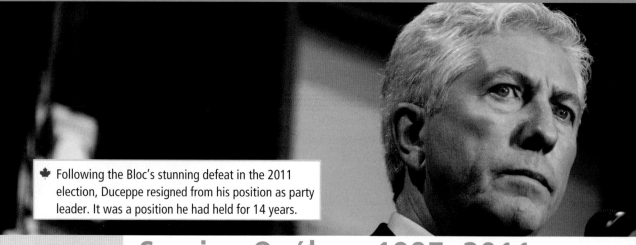

Following the Bloc's stunning defeat in the 2011 election, Duceppe resigned from his position as party leader. It was a position he had held for 14 years.

# Serving Québec, 1997–2011

In 1997, Prime Minister Jean Chrétien called a snap election. The Bloc Québécois' share of the popular vote in Québec fell to 38 per cent, and although it still captured 44 of the province's 75 seats, the Reform Party became the Official Opposition.

The victorious Liberal government asked the Supreme Court of Canada to decide if a province could legally separate from Canada. The Québec government boycotted the hearings. When the Supreme Court ruled that a province could separate from Canada if a "clear" majority voted "yes" on a "clear" question, both sides claimed victory.

In December 1999, the Liberal government introduced the Clarity Act. Based on the Supreme Court ruling, the Bill outlined the conditions under which the federal government would negotiate separation of a province. The Bloc fought to prevent the Bill from passing, but in 2000, it became law. The Clarity Act stated that no province could separate from Canada until its citizens voted yes on a clear referendum question.

In the November 2000 election, the Bloc again won 38 seats, but it rebounded in the 2004 election, winning 54 seats in the House of Commons. Since Paul Martin's Liberal Party failed to gain a majority of the seats, the Bloc, the NDP, and the Canadian Alliance Party now possessed more influence on government policies.

In November 2005, the Conservative Party, the NDP, and the Bloc passed a **motion of non-confidence** in the government, prompting an election early in 2006. The overall result of the election was a Conservative minority government.

When neither the Bloc nor the NDP agreed to work with the Harper government, the prime minister called an election for 2008 in hopes of forming a majority government. The plan did not work, and the Conservatives again formed a minority government. The Bloc fell two seats short of its 2006 results, and its share of the popular vote fell to the lowest ever.

Canadians went to the polls again in 2011. This election, however, witnessed a major shift in the political landscape of Québec, as the NDP captured 58 of the province's 75 seats. The Bloc was reduced to four seats and Gilles Duceppe, who lost his own seat, resigned as party leader. NDP leader, Jack Layton, courted the growing number of Québécois who did not want another referendum on sovereignty.

**The Clarity Act stated that no province could separate from Canada until its citizens vote yes on a clear referendum question.**

# TERMS OF SECESSION

In 1999, the federal government drew up the Clarity Act that outlined the conditions under which the federal government would negotiate separation of a province. This document made it clear that there was more to separating than a simple referendum vote. The terms of secession caused an uproar in Canadian politics. Some argued that a vote should be reason enough to leave the country. Others stated that separating from a country was not that simple.

## SEPARATION BY REFERENDUM

The Clarity Act was bitterly condemned by every provincial party in Québec. Lucien Bouchard and the Parti Québécois defined a clear majority vote as 50 percent plus one. Gilles Duceppe of the Bloc argued that "In a democracy, the people decide. In Québec, the Québécois must make decisions concerning their own future…."

## SEPARATION BY NEGOTIATION

The federal Liberal Party stated that 50 percent plus one was too small a majority to decide Canada's fate. The party felt that independence should be achieved through negotiation rather than a "unilateral declaration of independence." The federal government must play a major role in deciding what percent of the vote is required for secession.

## THE RESULT

The Clarity Act became law in June 2000. It stated that no province could separate from Canada until a clear majority of its citizens voted yes on a clear referendum question as determined by the House of Commons. The Québec separatist movement now lost its momentum.

**In 1998 the Supreme Court of Canada ruled that:**
1. It would be illegal for Québec to declare **unilateral** separation from Canada.
2. If the Québec people voted to separate in a provincial referendum, the Canadian government would be obliged to negotiate separation terms.
3. The referendum vote must be a clear majority.
4. The vote must be made on a clear question.

The Supreme Court was presented with three questions regarding the secession of a province. The questions referred to the legality of secession under Canada's Constitution and under international law, and asked which of the two had precedence if their answers were in conflict with each other.

The Clarity Act continued to anger Québecers for years. In November 2005, Bloc leader Gilles Duceppe met with Parti Québécois leader Andre Boisclair to discuss Québec's sovereignty. Boisclair stated that he intended to ignore the Clarity Act in any future referendums.

# TIMELINE

The Bloc Québécois has its foundation in events that occurred hundreds of years ago. This timeline highlights some of the key moments in Canadian history that ultimately led to the separatist movement and the formation of the Bloc into what it is today.

**1763**
Great Britain wins the Seven Years War and takes control of Québec.

**1763**
The Royal Proclamation sets forth plans to assimilate French Canadians.

**1791**
French Canadians are given their own colony called Lower Canada.

**1837**
French Canadians rebel against British influences.

**1839**

**1839**
Lord Durham releases his report recommending the creation of one province and the assimilation of French Canadians.

**1867**
Confederation separates the Province of Canada into Québec and Ontario.

**1885**
Louis Riel is hanged.

**1890**
The Manitoba Schools Act removes French-language instruction from the province's schools.

**1899–1902**
The Boer War

**1914–1919**
World War I

**1917**
The government begins conscription. Riots occur in Québec City and Montreal.

**1960**
The Quiet Revolution begins.

**1968**
The Parti Québécois is formed.

**1970**

The FLQ crisis takes place.

**1980**

Québec holds its first referendum on sovereignty.

**1982**

Canada's Constitution is patriated.

**1987**

**1990**

The Meech Lake Accord fails to pass.

Bouchard forms an informal coalition with disenchanted Québec MPs.

**1990**

Bloc candidate Gilles Duceppe wins a seat in the House of Commons.

**1991**

The Bloc Québécois becomes an official political party.

**1992**

The referendum on the Charlottetown Accord is held.

**1995**

Québec holds another referendum on sovereignty.

**1999**

The Clarity Act is passed.

# 10 FAST FACTS
# ABOUT THE BLOC QUÉBÉCOIS

**1** The Parti Québécois and the Bloc Québécois are two separate parties. However, they have similar goals and work together to achieve them.

**2** In the 2008 election, 15 women were elected as Bloc members. This was 30 percent of the party's MPs and was the highest number among the major parties.

**3** Supporters of the Bloc Québécois are called "Bloquistes."

**4** The Bloc's platform contains issues unrelated to sovereignty. It is a firm believer in the Kyoto Protocol and environmental policies. As part of its platform, the Bloc wants more incentives for the development of cleaner energy sources, such as wind and water, to discourage reliance on carbon-based sources. The party also wants mandatory labelling for foods with genetically modified organisms.

**5** In its 2008 election platform, the Bloc campaigned for its exclusion from the Canadian Multiculturalism Act. Multiculturalism encourages the immigration of different ethnic groups into the country and allows them to retain their unique cultural traditions and lifestyles. The Bloc feels this law is a threat to French language and culture.

**6** The Bloc has been instrumental in providing Québec with more control over provincial affairs. In Parliament, it has succeeded in returning control over labour training to the province. It has also given Québec control of parental leave programs. As well, it has been at least partly responsible for obtaining funding for provincial health care and social programs, and has helped Québec obtain millions of dollars in funding for its aeronautical industry.

**7** Gilles Duceppe led the Bloc for more than 10 years. At the time of the 2011 election, he was the longest running party leader on the Canadian political scene.

**8** Gilles Duceppe studied political science at the Université de Montréal but did not graduate. While in university, he was the general manager of the school's newspaper, *Quartier Latin*.

**10** The Bloc runs 75 candidates in federal elections. All of these candidates campaign for ridings in Québec.

**9** When first created, the Bloc Québécois was meant to be a temporary political party. It was to be dissolved when Québec sovereignty was achieved.

## ACTIVITY

# WHAT IS A DEBATE?

When people debate a topic, two sides take a different viewpoint about one idea. They present logical arguments to support their views. Usually, each person or team is given a set amount of time to present its case. The presenters take turns stating their arguments until the total time set aside for the debate is used up. Sometimes, there is an audience in the room listening to the presentations. Later, the members of the audience vote for the person or team they think made the most persuasive arguments.

Debating is an important skill. It helps people to think about ideas thoughtfully and carefully. It also helps them develop rhythms of speech that others can follow easily.

Some schools have organized debating clubs as part of their after-school activities. Schools often hold debates in their history class or as part of studying about world events.

# DEBATE THIS!

Every day, the news is filled with the issues facing Canada and its citizens. These issues are debated in the House of Commons and on city streets. People often have different views of these issues and support different solutions.

Following is an issue that has sparked discussion across the country. Gather your friends or classmates, and divide into two teams to debate the issue. Each team should take time to properly research the issue and develop solid arguments for their side.

The Bloc Québécois was created with the goal of achieving sovereignty for Québec. However, in recent years, talk of Québec separatism has declined, and the Bloc appears to have become one of Canada's mainstream political parties. Its goals seem more tied to representing the needs of Québec at the federal level than actual separation.

This raises the question to be debated:

Is the issue of Québec sovereignty relevant to Canada today?

# QUIZ

**1:** What is the chief goal of the Bloc Québécois?

**2:** Who was the Bloc's first leader?

**3:** When Great Britain gained control of Québec in 1791, how did it initially plan to deal with French Canadians?

**4:** What happened to the United Province of Canada following Confederation?

**5:** What was the Quiet Revolution?

**6:** How did Brian Mulroney plan to resolve Québec's issues?

**7:** When did the Bloc become an official political party?

**8:** How was the 1995 Québec referendum question different from those in the past?

**9:** What is the Clarity Act?

**10:** What is the Parti Québécois' relationship to the Bloc?

# FURTHER RESEARCH

## Suggested Reading

Bothwell, Robert. *Canada and Québec: One Country Two Histories*. Vancouver: University of British Columbia Press, 1998.

Jacobs, Jane. *The Question of Separatism*. Montreal: Baraka Books, 2009.

Charbonneau, Marie-France. *Bloc Québécois (Le): 20 ans au nom du Québec*. Montreal: Richard Vézina Editeur, 2011.

## Internet Resources

Read about the Bloc Québécois directly from the source at **www.blocQuébecois.org**

A detailed history of the Bloc Québécois can be found at **www.thecanadianencyclopedia.com**. Just type Bloc Québécois into the search engine.

Learn more about Canada's political parties and the election process at **www.elections.ca**

# GLOSSARY

**arms race:** the continuing competitive attempt by two or more nations each to have available to it more and more powerful weapons than the other

**assimilate:** gradually influence people from different backgrounds to become alike in customs and viewpoints

**autonomous:** self-governing; independent

**colonies:** regions ruled by a country that is usually far away

**conscription:** forced military service

**Constitution:** the set of principles and laws by which a nation is governed

**democratic:** based on a political system in which the people elect the members of their government

**dual citizenship:** the status of an individual who is a citizen of two or more nations

**Front de Libération du Québec (FLQ):** a terrorist organization seeking the secession of Québec from Canada, mainly active in the 1960s

**martial law:** temporary rule by military officials

**motion of non-confidence:** a vote to bring down the government

**nationalized:** converted from private to government ownership

**New France:** French possessions in North America, from the end of the 16th century to 1763, including parts of eastern Canada, the Great Lakes region, and the Mississippi Valley

**Parti Québécois:** a provincial political party in Québec that supports separatism

**patriate:** to bring under the control of an autonomous country

**ratified:** approved and gave formal sanction to

**referendum:** the submission of an issue of public importance to the direct vote of the electorate

**responsible government:** a form of government in which decisions cannot become law without the support of the majority of elected representatives

**secession:** the formal withdrawal from membership in an organization, association, or alliance

**sovereign nation:** a country that governs itself independently of any foreign power

**sovereignty-association:** a proposed arrangement by which Québec would become independent but would maintain a formal association with Canada

**unilateral:** decision by one side that affects others

**War Measures Act:** a Canadian statute that allowed the government to assume sweeping emergency powers in the event of war

# INDEX